Growing as a Christian

BOOK FOUR OF THE STUDIES IN CHRISTIAN LIVING

A MINISTRY OF THE NAVIGATORS
P.O. BOX 35001, COLORADO SPRINGS, COLORADO 80935

OUR GUARANTEE TO YOU

We believe so strongly in the message of our books that we are making this quality guarantee to you. If for any reason you are disappointed with the content of this book, return the title page to us with your name and address and we will refund to you the list price of the book. To help us serve you better, please briefly describe why you were disappointed. Mail your refund request to: NavPress, P.O. Box 35002, Colorado Springs, CO 80935.

The Navigators is an international Christian organization. Our mission is to reach, disciple, and equip people to know Christ and to make Him known through successive generations. We envision multitudes of diverse people in the United States and every other nation who have a passionate love for Christ, live a lifestyle of sharing Christ's love, and multiply spiritual laborers among those without Christ.

NavPress is the publishing ministry of The Navigators. NavPress publications help believers learn biblical truth and apply what they learn to their lives and ministries. Our mission is to stimulate spiritual formation among our readers.

At Milepost Four

If you have completed the first three books in <u>Studies in Christian Living</u>, you already know the profit of personal Bible study—what it means to search the Scriptures and come up with answers. You probably have noticed how God's word has affected your attitudes and actions day by day.

But even though you've seen the value of systematic Bible study, you probably will sense opposition as you continue. The enemy of every Christian, Satan himself, knows the power of God's word in your life and will try at every turn to keep you from it. He will suggest such excuses as, "You're too busy," or, "You can't concentrate now, so do something else first and get to Bible study later." He will engineer interruptions, temptations, and even criticism by others to hinder you from giving your attention to God's word.

Just recognizing that Satan is the source of such hindrances is helpful. It reemphasizes the importance of Bible study, and can spur your determination to gain victory.

How can you win this battle? Here are some suggestions.

First, accept by faith the victory Christ already has won over Satan and all his works. "Thanks be to God! He gives us the victory through our Lord Jesus Christ" (1 Corinthians 15:57).

Second, use personal discipline. No spiritual exercise is automatic. Just as you must make an effort to keep up your daily devotional time with God, so you must plan and zealously guard your study time.

Third, arrrange with a friend to check each other weekly on completed goals in Bible study, and perhaps share with each other something you have learned.

In this study book you will explore Christian character — what you as a Christian should aspire to be in Christ. The five chapter topics are:

- •Maturing in Christ
- •Demonstrating Christ
- •Developing Integrity
- •Growing in Discipleship
- •Obedience and Blessing

CHAPTER ONE

Maturing in Christ

Our New Life

1. What has God planned for us?

   Romans 8:29 _____

   _____

   Ephesians 1:4 _____

   _____

   1 Peter 2:9 _____

   _____

2. Which of these statements best summarizes the truth of
   1 John 2:5-6?

   ☐ We cannot live up to Christ's standards.
   ☐ Christians should live as Christ lived.
   ☐ Christians should avoid any unnecessary contact
   with the world.

3. According to these passages, what should our life in
   Christ be like?

   Galatians 5:16 _____

   _____

   Ephesians 5:1-2 _____

   _____

Ephesians 5:8 _____

_____

4. Where should our attention ultimately be focused?

   2 Corinthians 4:18 _____

   Colossians 3:1-2 _____

How We're Changed

5. Read Philippians 2:12-13. Who is at work in you?

   _____

   What is he doing?

   _____

   _____

6. According to 2 Corinthians 3:17-18, what kind of change are we undergoing?

   _____

   Who brings about this change?

   _____

   Is this change completed all at once?

   _____

7. Read Romans 12:2. What should you avoid?

   _____

   What should be happening to your mind?

   _____

   What will you then be able to do?

   _____

   _____

8. Study Ephesians 4:22-24. In what ways is your new self more like God?

_____

_____

_____

What should you do with your old self?

_____

_____

9. In Romans 13:13-14 we are given standards for not yielding to sin. Write out these verses in your own words. (Use a dictionary to look up any words you don't know.)

_____

_____

_____

_____

_____

_____

10. Read Romans 6:11-14. What should be your relationship to sin?

_____

_____

What decision should you therefore make about your body?

_____

_____

Reading and meditating on Romans 6:1-14 will help you learn more about dealing with sin's influence in your life.

11. What description is given in 2 Corinthians 5:7 of how we live our new life? (Check the best answer.)

☐ By confidence in our own abilities
☐ By sincerity and diligence
☐ By trusting in Christ and depending on him
☐ By clearly understanding major Bible doctrines

Faith

12. What is a basic requirement for pleasing God? (Hebrews 11:6)

_____

13. What happened to Abraham's faith? (Romans 4:20)

_____

14. How would you define faith from these passages?

Romans 4:20-21 _____

_____

Hebrews 11:1 _____

_____

_____

15. What does faith make possible? Match the following.

_____ Hope, joy, peace   a. Matthew 21:22
_____ Answered prayer   b. Romans 15:13
_____ Power over Satan   c. Ephesians 3:12
_____ Access to God   d. Ephesians 6:16

16. According to Matthew 6:25-32, what basic needs in your life can you trust God to provide for?

_____

_____

_____

17. Read James 1:2-4. How should we respond to trials?

_____

8

How does this affect our faith?

_____

_____

18. What godly characteristics accompany mature faith? (1 Timothy 6:11)

_____

_____

19. How many times is the word <u>faith</u> used in Hebrews 11?

_____

20. Read through Hebrews 11, and write out here your one or two favorite verses from this chapter.

_____

_____

_____

_____

_____

_____

How does the truth of these verses apply to your own life?

_____

_____

_____

_____

CHAPTER TWO

Demonstrating Christ

Love in Action

1. How does Paul describe love in Romans 13:10?

   _____

   _____

2. List the characteristics of love named in
   1 Corinthians 13:4-7.

   _____

   _____

   _____

   _____

   _____

   _____

3. What things are useless without love?
   (1 Corinthians 13:1-3)

   _____

   _____

   _____

   _____

4. What did Jesus say our love would demonstrate to the world? (John 13:34-35)

_____

_____

_____

5. What guidelines do these verses give about love?

Romans 12:9 _____

1 Corinthians 16:14 _____

1 John 4:21 _____

6. What is the basis for our love?

Romans 5:5 _____

_____

1 John 4:10 _____

_____

_____

7. Who should we love?

Mark 12:30 _____

Luke 6:27-28 _____

Ephesians 5:25 _____

Titus 2:3-4 _____

8. How should love be demonstrated? (1 John 3:17-18)

_____

_____

What does this mean to you?

_____

_____

_____

_____

Good Works

9. What purpose for our lives is stated in Ephesians 2:10?

_____

_____

10. According to these passages, why should we do good works?

    Matthew 5:16 _____

    _____

    Ephesians 6:7-8 _____

    _____

11. How did Peter describe Jesus' way of life in Acts 10:38?

    _____

    _____

12. Why did Paul commend Phoebe in Romans 16:1-2?

    _____

13. Read the list of commands related to Christian love and service in Romans 12:9-21. Which one or two of these is hardest for you to obey, and why?

    _____

    _____

    _____

    _____

    _____

    _____

    _____

14. What guideline for our service is given in Colossians 3:17?

    _____

    _____

15. Write out Galatians 6:9-10 in your own words.

_____

_____

_____

_____

_____

_____

_____

16. According to James 2:15-17, what serves as proof of whether our faith is alive?

_____

_____

Humility

17. How did Jesus Christ demonstrate humility? (Philippians 2:5-8)

_____

_____

18. According to these verses, what does God want in his people?

Proverbs 27:2 _____

_____

Micah 6:8 _____

_____

_____

Romans 12:3 _____

_____

_____

1 Peter 5:5 _____

_____

19. What is the result of being humble?

Psalm 25:9 _____

_____

Proverbs 29:23 _____

_____

James 4:10 _____

_____

20. What is the result of being proud?

Proverbs 11:2 _____

Proverbs 16:5 _____

21. Read Luke 14:7-11. What principle is Jesus teaching in this parable?

_____

_____

_____

22. Read Luke 22:24-27. What were the disciples arguing about?

_____

What example did Jesus remind them that he had set for them?

_____

_____

23. Write out Philippians 2:3-4 in your own words.

_____

_____

_____

14

_____

_____

_____

24. Review your answers in this chapter. Choose one verse
in each of the three sections ("Love in Action," "Good
Works," and "Humility") which to you is the most mean-
ingful verse in that section, and summarize here how it
impressed you:

Love in Action _____

_____

_____

Good Works _____

_____

_____

Humility _____

_____

_____

What step can you take to make one of these biblical
principles more evident in your life?

_____

_____

_____

_____

_____

_____

CHAPTER THREE

Developing Integrity

The Power of the Tongue

1. How is our tongue described in James 3:7-10?

   _____

   _____

   _____

   _____

2. What danger is mentioned in these verses?

   James 1:26 _____

   _____

   Proverbs 10:19 _____

   _____

3. For what good purposes can our speech be used?

   Psalm 35:28 _____

   _____

   Psalm 145:10-12 _____

   _____

   Isaiah 50:4 _____

   _____

4. What instruction does God give about our speech in these verses?

Proverbs 21:23 _____

_____

Ephesians 4:25 _____

_____

James 4:11 _____

_____

5. What does your speech indicate? (Matthew 12:34-35)

_____

_____

_____

6. What is characteristic of a foolish person, according to these verses from Proverbs?

15:2 _____

29:11 _____

7. According to these verses, what can gracious and appropriate words do?

Proverbs 12:25 _____

Proverbs 15:1 _____

Ephesians 4:29 _____

Read David's prayer in Psalm 141:3. Take a moment to pray this verse yourself, keeping in mind any specific ways in which you are often tempted to misuse your tongue.

How Important Is Purity?

8. What promise does Jesus make in Matthew 5:8 concerning the pure in heart?

_____

9. Which of these statements most accurately summarizes the standard God gives us in 1 Peter 1:14-16?

☐Live above the standard of today's society.
☐Follow the standards and example of other Christians.
☐God himself is our standard in all areas of life.
☐Avoid practices which you believe are wrong.

10. What is the source of our evil desires? (Mark 7:21-23)

_____

11. In Ephesians 4:18-19, how did Paul describe those who practice impurity?

_____

_____

_____

12. What are we told to avoid in Ephesians 5:3-4?

_____

_____

_____

13. Summarize what these passages say about why a Christian should avoid immorality.

1 Corinthians 6:15-20 _____

_____

_____

1 Thessalonians 4:7-8 _____

_____

_____

1 John 2:15-16 _____

_____

_____

14. What did David ask God for in Psalm 51:10?

_____

15. What guidelines are given in these verses on how to live a pure life?

Galatians 5:16 _____

2 Timothy 2:22 _____

_____

16. What can you do to avoid the things that tempt your mind away from God's standard for purity?

_____

_____

_____

_____

Why Be Honest?

17. What goal does Jesus give us in Luke 6:31?

_____

_____

18. What commands for integrity are given in these verses?

Leviticus 19:11 _____

_____

Leviticus 25:14 _____

_____

Deuteronomy 25:15-16 _____

_____

Romans 13:7 _____

_____

Ephesians 4:28 _____

_____

19. What did Jesus say about Satan's integrity in John
    8:44?

_____

_____

20. According to Colossians 3:9-10, why should we speak
    honestly?

_____

21. Read Hebrews 4:13. Why is it useless to try deceiving
    God?

_____

_____

22. Read Acts 24:16. In whose eyes did Paul intend to have
    a clear conscience?

_____

    Did this require effort on his part?

_____

23. Do you need to take a step of action now to correct
    some dishonesty on your part in the past? If so, list here
    what you will do.

_____

_____

_____

_____

CHAPTER FOUR

Growing in Discipleship

Diligence and Discipline

1. What guidelines for work are given in Colossians 3:23-24?

   _____

   _____

2. Write Proverbs 13:4 in your own words.

   _____

   _____

   _____

   _____

3. Read 2 Chronicles 31:20-21. What was the result of Hezekiah's faith and wholehearted work?

   _____

   _____

4. What observations about laziness are given in these verses?

   Proverbs 18:9 _____

   Proverbs 21:25 _____

   Ecclesiastes 10:18 _____

5. Read Ephesians 5:15-16. What should we do with our time?

_____

_____

6. Study 1 Corinthians 9:24-27. What factors are important for successfully running the Christian race?

_____

_____

_____

_____

Suffering

7. What kind of suffering is Jesus speaking about in Luke 6:22-23?

_____

_____

How should we respond when we experience this kind of suffering?

_____

Why should we respond this way?

_____

_____

8. In 1 Peter 2:19-20, what kind of situation is said to be pleasing to God?

_____

_____

9. Summarize what 1 Peter 2:21-23 teaches about the example Christ left us.

_____

_____

10. In John 15:18-19, Jesus told his disciples to expect the world's hatred for what reason?

_____

_____

11. According to these passages, why does God allow us to experience hardship?

Hebrews 12:5-7 _____

_____

1 Peter 1:6-7 _____

_____

12. Read Romans 12:19. Why should we not seek revenge when we suffer?

_____

_____

13. What attitudes toward suffering did these men demonstrate?

The apostles (Acts 5:41) _____

_____

Stephen (Acts 7:59-60) _____

_____

Moses (Hebrews 11:24-26) _____

_____

14. Read Psalm 119:67 and 119:71. How did this man benefit from suffering?

_____

_____

15. What other benefits from suffering are taught in these passages?

2 Corinthians 1:3-4 _____

_____

2 Corinthians 4:16-17 _____

Hebrews 12:11 _____

Discovering God's Will

16. What conditions for finding God's will are given in
    Romans 12:1-2?

    _____

    _____

    _____

17. What do we learn in these verses about the part Scrip-
    ture plays in our understanding God's guidance?

    Psalm 37:30-31 _____

    _____

    Psalm 119:105 and 119:130 _____

    _____

18. What step for understanding God's will is taught in
    James 1:5-6?

    _____

    _____

19. How does the Holy Spirit help us learn God's will?
    (John 16:13)

    _____

    _____

20. In seeking God's will, what attitudes taught in Proverbs
    3:5-6 should we hold toward God?

    _____

    _____

21. Read Ephesians 5:21—6:4. What is God's will for:

Wives? _____

_____

Husbands? _____

_____

Children? _____

_____

Fathers? _____

_____

22. What truth about God's will for us did Jesus teach in Matthew 6:33?

_____

_____

23. What passages from this chapter impressed you most, and why?

_____

_____

_____

_____

What step can you take to apply the truth of one of these passages to your life?

_____

_____

_____

_____

CHAPTER FIVE

Obedience and Blessing

Following Christ

1. In John 6:38, what did Jesus say was his purpose on earth?

   _____

2. In John 14:15, what did Jesus say was the test of our love for him?

   _____

3. According to 1 John 2:3-4, what else do we demonstrate by obeying the Lord's commands?

   _____

   _____

4. What results of obeying God's truth are mentioned in 1 Peter 1:22?

   _____

   _____

5. Read Matthew 7:24-27, in which Jesus illustrates what happens to those who approach his words in either of two ways. What is the difference between these two responses to his teaching?

   _____

   _____

6. Read Romans 13:1-2. Why should we obey government authorities?

_____

_____

7. According to Hebrews 13:17, why should we obey spiritual leaders?

_____

_____

8. What did Peter teach about obedience in 1 Peter 2:18-19?

_____

_____

9. In these verses, what does Jesus promise to anyone who obeys him?

John 14:23 _____

John 15:10 _____

John 15:14 _____

10. Read the Ten Commandments in Exodus 20:1-17. Summarize here what each one says to you.

(1) (verse 3) _____

_____

(2) (verses 4-6) _____

_____

(3) (verse 7) _____

_____

(4) (verses 8-11) _____

_____

(5) (verse 12) _____

_____

(6) (verse 13) _____

_____

(7) (verse 14) _____

_____

(8) (verse 15) _____

_____

(9) (verse 16) _____

_____

(10) (verse 17) _____

_____

11. What did Jesus say were the greatest and the second greatest commandments? (Matthew 22:34-40)

_____

_____

_____

12. According to these passages, what attitudes should characterize our obedience?

Deuteronomy 26:16 _____

Joshua 1:9 _____

Psalm 40:8 _____

13. What does Psalm 119:59-60 teach about obeying God's commands?

_____

Examples of Obedience

14. Read Luke 5:1-11, in which Jesus asked Peter to do something that contradicted Peter's best judgment. Why did Peter obey Jesus?

_____

What was the result for Peter of his obedience?

_____

_____

_____

15. Read Hebrews 11:8-10. What did Abraham do in obedience to God?

_____

_____

Why did he obey?

_____

_____

16. Read Genesis 22:1-18. How did Abraham obey God in this passage?

_____

_____

What was the result of his obedience?

_____

_____

17. In Acts 13:22, what did God say about David?

_____

_____

Dangers of Disobedience

18. Read Zechariah 7:8-14. How did the people respond to God's instruction?

_____

_____

_____

How did this affect their prayers?

_____

What else happened to them?

_____

_____

19. Is there a specific area in your life in which you
believe God wants you to exercise closer obedience?
If so, how can you do this?

_____

_____

_____

_____

_____

_____

Turn your small group from just a bunch of people to a tightly knit community.

Does your small group feel like just a bunch of people? Do you long for greater intimacy and growth?

With Pilgrimage/NavPress Small-Group Training Seminars you can turn your small group into a community of believers excited to study God's Word and apply it to their lives. With new leadership skills and practical "how to" help, you'll be equipped to provide well-trained leadership and direction for your group, turning it from just a bunch of people to a community that supports and cares for one another.

Here's what you'll learn.

You'll learn ►how trends within society set the stage for small groups ►how you can use the four primary phases of group development to guarantee the right fit for every small-group member ►seven ways to cultivate a caring atmosphere ►five common problems to avoid ►the six foundational elements of every small group ►and much, much more!

Space is limited. Call (800) GRPS-R-US today for more information about seminars in your area.

(800) 477-7787, ask for offer **#303**

**PILGRIMAGE
NAVPRESS**
www.navpress.com